This Too Shall Pass.......

By

Sunshine

THE JOURNEY TO HEALING

This book has some continuation from my autobiography book: Looking In From The Outside along with society issues. Come and take a walk with me and my healing progress. I have been lied on, cheated on, disrespected, threatened, hated on, divorce, child support issues, court, racism and so much more.

I pray my stories help you in your healing journey as well. I have endured so much through my life but the blessings that have now started hitting my house are amazing.

The Process:

Listen, the process is hard. God will only show you the result but not the process because it will scare you. The attacks, the lies, the deceit, the manipulative people, the firing, the ups and downs. I say this because it's all true but at the end of the process you come out looking like Pure Gold.

Don't allow your circumstances now make you forget the end results GOD has shown you. If you are doing what God says to do, then at the end YOU WIN.

Trust me, I know it's not easy! Trust me, I know you think you're not going to make it. I have faith in God, so I know if He sent me to do an assignment- it's already won! Just follow His instructions and watch Him work!

Life

Where do I begin when it comes to life? Life throws so many curve balls at us and sometimes it's hard to catch our breath. Well, I am here to tell you, you got this! No matter what life throws at you. Stand tall with your head held high and don't you dare give up!

Trials come to make us stronger, see the weak spots and sharpen them to never face that same issue again. If it happens again at least you know how to handle it the second time around.

Don't let life break you! Don't let people break you! Don't allow life to beat you up!

THIS TOO SHALL PASS......WHEW THIS TITLE ALONE WILL HAVE MANY TOPICS POP UP IN YOUR MIND. THIS BOOK I AM ADDRESS MANY MORE ISSUES THAT NEED TO BE SPOKEN OUT LOUD. IT IS TIME FOR A CHANGE AND THE TIME IS NOW!

LET'S HEAL....... LET'S DISCUSS IT....... LET'S GROW FOR THE BETTER......

POETRY

I Choose ME!

I choose me this time around!

I'm putting my foot down and not allowing you to put me down!

I choose me!

No more being disrespected or dismissed

I have finally figured out what love is about!

I love me and refuse to be put second to none!

Always putting others first before me and making sure they were good.

My happiness is important to me.

I value me above all else

Yes, I deserve to be happy just like everyone else.

So why should I be placed on the back burner, just to feed your ego?

I CHOOSE ME!

It's Me Again

It's me again asking you where have you been
Did you forget about me once again?
About that promise that you made me
I waited all day for you
Why are you making me feel so blue?
I cry every time you pass me by
I thought I was supposed to be your angel in your eyes
Your baby girl
The one your supposed to come home running to
But, instead of showing me your love you, just placed me to the side
So you can go out and ride the streets
What must I do to get your attentions?
Fall at your feet and see if you will respond to me
It's too late to spend that father and daughter time together
I have so much anger towards you
That I cannot stand you like I cannot stand this cold weather
Now you're telling me that I am making you blue
Oh well... who knew?
That the same pain that you caused me
Is now bringing me the victory
It's too late to show your grace
God has now dealt you a hand that you cannot even face
Look at me while I tell you this
Face to face
Now, now don't start crying now
I'm not gonna show you any remorse

Follow me

Follow me and you shall see
What life can be made of
Do not say no until I show you
How good it can be
If only you let me
Do not hide because it will only find you
You cannot run from your life
Because then you will be living tiff
And then you will see the bad side of life
Please don't do that to yourself

HEAVEN ABOVe

Heaven shows everyone love and affection
All you need is that direction
I will show you the way
But, I am not ready to stay
I have my son to look after
Each and everyday
He's my love of my life
And I will place no one above him
For he is my pride and joy
He brings sunshine and laughter to me
Without him I do not know where I would be
<u>GOOD BYE</u>
DADDY ROY
When the sunrises
I see your eyes
I see your smile
I hear you laugh
When the sun goes down
I see you frown
So I look down
And make a frown
I hear your voice
Telling me goodbye
You say you will
See me another day
But for now its goodbye
But you say
Never cry

Because your always around
If so then why do I have this frown
And
Why do I feel so down?

If you were here

Dad
If you were here
I would hold you tight!
I would never let you go
If you were here
There would be tears from my eyes
If you were here, I could tell you how much
I love you
That's if you were here!

<u>Reflections of a LOVE RELATIONSHIP</u>

Do you remember the first time we met?
Solely by coincidence, something meant to be
Do you ever think of our first kiss & does it touch your memory
The same as it touches my thoughts
And what about our first day spent and earned;
A value worth a million memories
And please say you remember our first night
And let it strike your thoughts
The way it strikes my heart
Do you remember the first time we fought?
Inevitable and undeniable
You may even remember our making up
Also inevitable, due to the love between us
And don't forget the numbered fights that followed
Not something I wished to be, but was.
I remember...
I remember many times,
Many moments,
Many hours...
..... still to few
The good, the bad, the undefined!
All of it... remembered
And still yet, I wish there were more!

Depression

When I am depressed, I know you care
My sweet love you are there
Your so sweet & kind
Its you that I adore
It is you my heart cares for
My love is only for you
My dreams are just between me and you
When the sunshine's I think about you
The love I have for you grows deep inside
When I was crying I looked to my side and by my side there you are
when I looked at you, I smile
When I look at you I wanna cry
Those are happy tears not sad ones
I cry because I have so much love for you inside
When I must leave your side then that is why I cry now those are sad
tears saying goodbye.

FRIENDS

A friend is someone who will be there for you
One who will listen to you
Whenever you may be feeling blue
All you really need is to have a friend like you
It is good to have a friend like you
You have been there for me
That is very true
It is good to know that I can count on you

FAMILY

DIFFERENT TYPES OF FAMILIES

In today's world family comes in many different forms if you ask me. I will tell you what family means to me and then you can choose which category you fall under.

1. Blood related family: you are related by blood relations from your mother or father's side.
2. Friends of the family: your parents have had dealings/ relationships with that person for years and consider that person part of the family. In our family if someone has been there for you or your real family through thick and thin. Then you are not a friend but a family member to us.
3. Married into the family: you do not carry any form of blood relation, but you married into our family. We consider you family because of the union.
4. Sport Families: your children, teammates & parents. You are either on the court or field daily. You now become family lending a helping hand.

<u>NEVER DISRESPECT A PERSON THAT MAKES SURE YOU WAS GOOD WHEN NOBODY ELSE DID! REMEMBER IF SOMEONE IS MAKING SURE YOUR GOOD WITH EXPECTING NOTHING IN RETURN, THEN THAT PERSON SHOULD BE CONSIDERED FAMILY.</u>

Now do you see why I say we have many different categories on families. Now allow me to go further when speaking on families. The real definition on families in the webster dictionary states: persons of common ancestry, parents, children, group of related individuals. Now I will break each one down even further.

Blood Relatives- you can not choose what family you were born into, but you make the best out of what your born into. Now being related does not mean you get along with all family members. I can honestly say I do not get along with all my family members and I am ok with that. I do not associate myself with anyone who does not value the meaning of family & loyalty. I have family members who still talk to my evil ex-husband, some who have bullied me growing up and just talked straight behind my back. I do not want that nor need that in my life. Family is supposed to have each other's back and never let outsider's infiltrate. If you allow outsiders to infiltrate and cause discord between the families, then they must go period. I was raised by a village and rule number one in our family from the elders was: **YOU NEVER GO AGAINST YOUR BLOOD RELATIVES. ALWAYS HAVE EACHOTHERS BACKS because the outsiders should never win.** That is a family code, and I will always be true to that. Now if we are family and you have always shown you did not care about me then I make sure I stay my distance because that type of energy cannot enter my circle. Once someone shows me them, I believe them and keep mental notes.

For example: I have an aunt that my children have never met and if it is up to me, they will never meet her. As a child she would always make fun of the mole I was born with on the bottom of my chin. Growing up I was being teased in school about it and great a complex about the mole but then to have my aunt call it a dirt spot on my chin every chance she could. Now that caused more of a complex as a child with me. I addressed her numerous times and so did my mother to the point I told my mother I never wanted to be around her ever again. It is sad that growing up you see the jealousy of family members and for the family members to be cruel to innocent children. I made a vow when I was a child that my aunt was never welcomed in my home because she is still cruel to others to this day. Who does that to a child and makes fun of their niece knowing she has a self-complex about her birth mark? I could never understand it and I have stopped trying to figure people out. Rule number one in my house, no bullies, no jealousy and you have each other's back or you're not staying in my circle. It is bad enough that I must deal with the outside world being cruel, but I do not have to accept it in my home or family.

Friends of the Family: now that I have many of them and I consider them family because they have proven themselves to me through the years and never wavered. I am forever loyal to them because they stay loyal to me. The Dennis Family are the first people I can say stay true to this since my oldest was 2 years old. We are still friends/family til this very moment. I love The Dennis Family and value them. We may go for months of not speaking because of our busy schedules but at the end of the day when we speak, we just pick up from where we left off. I cherish our friendship and I will drop what I am doing if they ever called stating they needed me.

Married into the Family: listen if the divorce was brutal and nasty then then your family needs to cut ties also. I do not care what anyone says. Loyalty is everything. You cannot keep in touch with my ex-especially when I finally tell everyone the reasons why we are now divorced. If any of them hang out or keep in contact with him. I cut them off. Rule number one LOYALTY and my ex should not know any of my business. I already have trust issues because of the hell I was put through growing up and in that seventeen-year relationship/thirteen-year marriage. So, if anyone says you guys are family you cannot disassociate yourself. Well, I am here to tell you I will, and I have done exactly that, disassociate myself from the rotten apples in the family. You cannot play on both sides of the fence with me. Nope my mental health and wellbeing is very crucial to me. I have full peace and I refuse to lose that ever again. I value me and my life.

Sports Family: my youngest plays basketball and baseball all year round. So, we stay more on the court and fields. The children my son plays with have become like our extended family. It's like a brotherhood and bonds have been formed. I love the friendships they have created, and it gets stronger each year. We help each other out by carpooling, tending to their needs on the field and off. The coaches treat the children as their own and want nothing but the best for them. I would not change the team dynamics.

I'M OLD SCHOOL

I was raised with a village, and I am so thankful about having so many family members loved me and taught me. The manners that were instilled in me are now being passed down to my children and granddaughter.

1. Whenever you enter someone's home, you always speak to everyone in the home.
2. Passing someone in the grocery store isle you say excuse me
3. Ladies don't call the men all the time because the man is supposed to Pursue the female.
4. Elbows off the table
5. Chew with your mouth closed
6. Answer an adult Yes or No Sir/Mame
7. Learn how to cook
8. Make sure your chores are done before leaving the house.
9. Do not have any dishes in the sink before going to bed.
10. Clean up behind yourself
11. Always look a person in the eyes with your shoulders straight up
12. Keep your promises because your word means everything
13. When entering a house, a man should always take off their hat
14. A gentleman should hold open the doors for a lady
15. Men should help carry the groceries in for the lady
16. Never let anyone disrespect your mother
17. Take the garbage out
18. Clean the house with CLOROX it kills germs
19. Don't ever Quit
20. Can't is not to be used in the house! Can't is like a curse word....
21. Value people who value you
22. Always treat people the way you would like to be treated
23. Be polite

24. Help others who are in need without looking for anything in return
25. Remember someone is always worse off than you so make the best out of each day.
26. Never make fun of anyone
27. Never Bully anyone
28. Step in if someone is getting bullied
29. Give back to your community
30. Protect your family
31. Always do your own research
32. Trust God in everything
33. Pay close attention to people's actions and not their words
34. Never eat with your back to the door
35. Your house comes first before anyone or anything outside of the home
36. Don't allow anyone to speak negative into you
37. Always try to be the best version you want to be
38. Always pay your debts- don't owe anyone anything
39. Character means everything!
40. Don't hang around people that's not going places. Never become complacent/stagnant.
41. Make sure you keep open communication with your children.
42. Watch who your children hang around and meet their parents.
43. Always make sure you carry $100 in your pocket in case anything happens.

These are life lessons and words to live by. Install these things in your family and reach for success. These are valuable teachings, and I am so thankful my family drilled this into me. Family values and old school teaching is the best way to go.

<u>A MOTHERS LOVE</u>

A mother's love is unbreakable, a never-ending commitment to loving, protecting, educating her child. We carry a child in our bodies for nine months. During those times we are already on guard in many aspects. We are now watching what we eat, what exercises we are conducting to keep our body in shape, making sure our behavior does not harm our unborn child in any situation. Women have been giving birth since GOD created us. Women were created to bring in new life into the world and that creates many more blessings. Not everyone can carry a child or even conceive, so it is truly a blessing to be able to carry a child and give birth. I treasure being a mother because when I look at my sons, I see me in them and my blood flows through their body. Flesh of my flesh really speaks volumes once you have your child placed in your arms after giving birth.

Once a child is placed in your arms it's a feeling that is indescribable because you have so many emotions running through you, but the most important emotion is that love. I do not know what it is but inside a switch clicks and it activates you to want to protect, love and cherish every part of that child until your last breath leaves your body. Well, I can only speak for myself, but I feel many mothers can agree with me on what I am writing. The most important job on this earth is our children besides ourselves. We want to make sure our family is well taken care of and well educated because our children represent us, and we represent them. What I mean by that is everything our children do outside of our home speaks volumes on how much the parents have taught, loved that child etc. The child is a reflection of the parents. Let me clarify and break down what I mean by that.

A Mothers first responsibility once that child is conceived is to do the best we can for that child. We want to show that child unconditional love, letting that child know that when the world mistreats them, they know they have someone who has their back. Mothers want to shield their children from anything that would try to typically break our children mentally or physically. Mothers are the momma bears in this world who will go to war to make sure their child is not hurt. Well, I can only speak for myself in that regard. I will go to war with anyone who has ill intentions.

Well, I can only speak for myself in that regard. I will go to war with anyone who harms my child or tries too.

MOTHER...... My version of a mother and who I am to my children......

A mother who will give her life for the precious cargo God granted her. A mother will go through morning sickness, surgery or whatever else that comes her way to bring a precious soul into this world! A mother will always reassure her precious GEMBS that they are worth it, loved and be their #1 fan in all aspects of their lives.

I am that mother! I love being a mother to my three sons because GOD entrusted me with them. No matter what age they get, I will always be there for them unconditionally. They will always be my babies and I will protect them as much as I possibly can. I will always be their biggest supporter. I will always pray for them and have their backs at any given time.

Now that is my version of what a mother should be, but sad to say I know many children who are growing up with a person they call mother but missing the protection, love, guidance and most important nurturing female aspect in their life. Some have never had a mother or a mother figure in their life.

Babies are not asked to be born into this world, so why should they suffer? Not everyone is meant to be a mother, and many want to have children but unfortunately some are barren and are unable to have children.

If you are not ready to be a parent, then please be responsible and strap it up and get on birth control. Better yet do not have sex till you are ready. Life is precious cherish what GOD gives you. Babies are gifts and deserve to be treasured but raised properly.

Can I ask you readers to participate: If you ever come across a child that needs a mother figure or just needs motherly love. Can you please show it to that child. One person can make a big difference in a child's life. Let's do better and show compassion towards everyone.

<u>DON'T START NONE</u>
<u>WON'T BE NONE</u>

Don't start none won't be none has always been the motto we say to anyone that tries to mess with us in our family. Let me make this very clear to everyone that is reading this book and that truly knows me. I do not start with people but if they come my way with the drama, I give them a warning first. If the person does not heed my warning, oh well they will soon find out, I am the wrong person to start drama with. I do not start nor look for drama but if it presents itself drama self towards me, I handle it.

I was raised to always walk away & turn the other cheek. Now my momma did say if someone puts their hands on you, then handle them a full course butt whoopin. So, you would think that the people around me would warn outsiders not to mess with my bottom line. Well, my ex-husband (Red Flag2) was doing malicious, vindictive things towards me and the low-level gutter rat (Jezebel 2) he was dating joined in.

Now side note: If I have an issue with someone, I take it to that person. Many can witness me pulling up on someone. I am woman enough to come to someone. I do not sugar coat anything. I speak my mind freely and I do not care who you are or what size you are.

Well, my ex-husband (Red Flag 2) did not want me and the gutter rat to talk (Jezebel 2). I told him to cut out the nonsense and put her in her place because she is not the children's mother. My sons have only one mother and that is how it will stay. My children will call me mom and no one else. Well Red Flag 2 kept doing sneaky things, having her live in the house while my children was with him for the week etc.

A situation with my middle son heartbeat 2 was the lead actor in the musical for his junior year of high school. Every year we place ads in the booklet for the musical. Well, red flag 2 took it upon himself to have a photo of jezebel 2, jezebel two children and my two sons in the phone stating I am so proud of you and we love you. This chick overstepped big time with that because allegedly they were only dating for 6 months by this time (which is a lie) and she had no right posting anything in my son's booklet. She is nothing to them and I flipped. I called her and told her that was the last straw and I needed her to stay in her place. I told her she had no right to post anything with my sons in the booklet. She is a no body and still a no body. I then flipped on red flag 2 and told him that he crossed my bottom line for the last time. I told him I tried hard to co-parent but every step of the way he was doing some evil towards me or the boys and this was the last straw.

The next day red flag 2 kept calling my phone while I was at work, and I kept sending him to voicemail because now it is war. I was fed up with him calling my phone so during my lunch break I answered the call and placed it on speaker. I am a paralegal and work in a law firm, so I wanted everyone to hear him and see the real red flag 2 and not the act he puts on while in public. Well red flag 2 showed his true colors and he did not know I had others listening. That low life red flag 2 called me all types of names and then jezebel 2 chimed in and made an open threat to me telling me she was coming to my job to kick my ass. I told red flag 2 that he was a piece of scum and then I told jezebel 2 I double dare her to come to my job because I have been wanting to whoop her slutty self from day one. I told her I knew she was the mistress and all I need her to do is to put one finger on me so I can make her a prime example for Buffalo to know I am not playing no games with anyone. I have turned the other cheek for too long. Too many people got comfortable with how they were speaking or treating me, and I HAD ENOUGH. I told them both that if she showed up, I would beat her down like she stole something and then press charges on her. They thought I was playing. Don't come for me unless I send someone to retrieve you. Understand just because I have walked away from people and their foolishness does not mean I have not wanted to smack and punch a few people. I am HOLY but also HOOD. Stop testing my patience. I then hung up and I called my uncle. My uncle told me to go to the police department now and press charges. I sure did press charges and I asked for a restraining order for both. Again, I tell everyone I love all but once you come for me, it is a wrap for anyone that threatens me.

You would think people would learn when they have a case coming up against them to fall back and not keep causing more drama. Well not these two idiots. Red flag 2 and Jezebel 2 both had the nerve to try and press charges against me. They had no leg to stand on in court and the judge threw the case out. The judge did not even know how a case against me appeared due to the fact I was the one who had a restraining order against them. Again, the elevator for these two did not go past the 1st floor. Anyways after dealing with their stupid tactics the judge granted me a full order of protection and restraining order against both of them. When I tell you I am done dealing with foolishness and evil people. Do not start any drama with me and then try to cry wolf. Red Flag 2 didn't stop there, he started lying to our sons and I had to break everything down for them on how the courts work. I advised how I had proof and witnesses that I could count on them calling me and threatening me. I never once threatened them until they came for me. Once you come for me it is over because I keep receipts, written documents and everything. I made sure the case would stick and I wanted them to get jail time. I told them both to stay clear of me and if they do not obey the court order, I will have them arrested real quick fast and in a hurry. I am the mother of his children and I make sure that our children are well taken care of and for him to call me disrespecting me was the last straw. We are now enemies, and I did not want that, but it is what it is. He started the war, and I am finishing it!

I wanted Red Flag 2 and I to co-parent in peace. I was the only one trying and for that first year he made it difficult every step of the way. So now I do not care one bit about co-parenting. My main concern as always is my children. If my children are safe, they are happy, that is all I care about. I keep my peace, joy and elevation regarding my career going.

My children now see who the cause of everything and I must keep reminding them that I want them to love both me and their father. They admit they have caught their father lying numerous times and they even apologized to me because of it. I told them never apologize for someone else's behavior. I tell them that their father needs to be accountable for his actions and I will make sure that it happens. I will not turn a blind eye to anyone that tries to mistreat me. I do not care who you are, no one will ever mistreat me again and think that it is ok because it is not. I no longer turn the other cheek and I no longer stay quiet. My peace means everything, and I love it.

Parents should co-parent properly for the children and keep adult issues away from the children. It is sad that it did not happen for us. One person vindictive and the other person trying as usual to be the peace maker. It does not work when both parties do not want to make it work in peace.

SIDE NOTE: It takes a lot for me to reciprocate the disrespect that is shown towards me. I warn people that I am not the one they want to try because there is only so much, I will walk away from before I come back to that party and give them the full blown 10 times worse. So, I tell people to stay in their lane and if I do not send for them to not even come my way. I mind my own business but baby if you come out of pocket towards me, you will catch the worst enemy ever. We are not the same. No one will be able to handle my response to any disrespect. Sometimes I do want to reciprocate people's disrespect but then I do take a few moments and evaluate how their life is going. Sometimes that alone is enough of a punishment but then again it depends on how I am disrespected. So again, be careful how you come to me because baby I am HOLY, but I am also HOOD when I need to be. Approach with caution.

<u>CO-PARENTING</u>

This is a hard topic to discuss but it really needs to be addressed. So many people have different values and different mindsets on how to parent the children after the relationship with the parents has ended. I am going to give my thoughts on how I wanted CO-PARENTING for my children after the ugly divorce. I spoke to many parents to get their point of view on CO-PARENTING and how they do it. After being married for 13 long years but being with that person for over 17 years. I knew this was going to be a hard situation, especially for the children.

1. **No one makes decisions about the children but the two parents. Other outside sources should not have a say!**
2. **Don't interfere with the other parent trying to be in the child's life.**
3. **Don't involve the children in the adult drama**
4. **People should love the children more than disliking the other parent**
5. **It is a process, and you must find what works for both parents**
6. **Try to make it a smooth transition for the children**
7. **Communicate properly with each other so no translation gets lost in the process**
8. **Be civil to each other in front of the children and out of sight**
9. **Both need to be mature and have adult conversations**

For me CO-PARENTING means everything I listed above. I wish we could have done this but when one parent is immature/vindictive it will not work. I pray he wakes up and realizes all the damage he has caused.

CHILD SUPPORT

Child support to me is supposed to be used for anything that contributes to helping the children. The child support can be used to pay rent, but food, clothes, sports, fun activities, utilities for the home.

DIVORCE

We do not ever get married to think about divorce. Unfortunately divorce happens and that's when all hell will break out in the dynamics. It's sad that things end but sometimes it's the best thing in life because why stay married to someone that does not love you, does not respect you and basically not honoring their vows. Never stay in a marriage that is loveless and disrespect is shown or given out. Value yourself enough to walk away and love yourself.

Now let's get to helping you prepare for the war that will begin once you agree on the divorce.

1. Make sure you are saving your money because the assets will now be put on hold until everything is sorted out and divided properly.
2. Make sure to write out all the assets that was yours before the marriage and what was gained together in the marriage. (Trust me this is very necessary)
3. If you have children find out if you're gonna split the children for shared custody or one parent having the child fully and the other parent just gets visitation for vacations and weekends.
4. If you have a house together: will you buy that person out? Will you sell the house and split the profit?
5. Start looking for a house or apartment to move into.
6. Sit down with the children and discuss what is going on in the house.
7. Get a therapist to talk with because emotions will be all over the place.

<u>CHURCH</u>

First Calvary Missionary Baptist Church was my church home for the past twelve years and that all came to an end during the nasty divorce. It was a painful decision, but I had to do what was best to keep my peace and to also not catch a case. Red Flag 2 had the nerve to bring his mistress jezebel 2 to our church that we have been going to for the past twelve years. This ninja would not stop being so evil and vindictive but when I saw them, I saw red and wanted to beat them both down. I am transparent and honest. Anyone that threatens to do physical harm to me and mistreats my children will always be an enemy of mine. You can never come back to the other side. No one and I mean no one threatens me or mistreats my children and think it's ok. The crazy thing people was believing all his lies except the Judge and District Attorney because I had proof and witnesses. Anyways let's get back to the church.

So, I did not have church hurt I had people hurt issues and I wanted to really lay holy hands on all those liars and gossipers, but GOD told me to keep my peace. God said I can leave the church and get a new church home. I am not going to lie when I say this, but it did hurt walking away from First Calvary Missionary Baptist Church but then I thought God is where I go, and HE is within me so why was I upset.

I now go to Tabernacle of Praise and when I say I love it. My pastor allows me to be fully free to worship and do what GOD instructs me to do. I am loving it, but it did take me a few months to get used to going to the new church. I keep in touch with some of the members at the other church, but the rest can KICK ROCKS. Anyone that got amnesia on all that I did for them with a genuine heart and how I never switched up on them but believed that Red Flag 2, yeah, I said it... they can KICK ROCKS and keep it moving. Now that they read my first book and my truth, now they want to call and text. Nope keep that same energy that you had during the divorce.

Before you ask if I am a Christian, I am and I forgive but I do not forget. Jesus flipped some tables and did not say be a fool and let them back in. So, listen to what I am say. The church did not hurt me the people that went to First Calvary Missionary Baptist Church hurt me and it's all good. Now that Red Flag showed his full hand and got married to the jezebel not even a year being divorced. People are now seeing all along it was Red Flag 2 who was cheating and out here lying on me. But again, they already chose sides instead of being neutral so for that, they can stay away from me fully and completely.

Remember GOD sees all and knows all, and everyone will reap what they sow. Red Flag 2 and Jezebel 2 will get what is coming to me, but it won't be by my hands. I turned them over to God as He fights my battles. GOD will handle anyone who mistreats his children. I was mistreated, disrespected and most of all lied on.

God said I will prepare a table in front of your enemies and have them watch me elevate you right in front of them. I said GOD have your way. Ever since I gave my life back to GOD in my early 30's, I know who fights my battles. GOD is my backup, and HE has not left my side. I am HIS daughter, and HE loves me unconditionally and I am so thankful to be called HIS.

Be careful who you mistreat because GOD will make you have to go back to the one you mistreated for assistance. Never put your mouth on one of GODS children. Think twice before gossiping and not knowing exactly what happened. Don't bring destruction to your home because your mouth got you in trouble.

I stand behind every word I said and if you do not believe me, read your bible.

<u>TRUST ISSUES</u>

What does trust mean? Per the dictionary, Trust means: firm belief in the reliability, truth, ability, or strength of someone or something. Trust issues means fear of betrayal, abandonment or manipulation. If one or both partners question the other's activities, words or actions. Trust issues come when people have lied to you repeatedly. Promises being broken throughout your lifetime. Yes, it is hard to trust but I am still out here willing to try it again on trusting people, just not the same ones that have let me down repeatedly. Now I will not tolerate it. I refuse to be disrespected in any aspect again: lied too, betrayed, my feelings not being heard and respected. For me personally, trust is more valuable than love because of one simple fact- you can't love someone you don't trust. If I don't trust you, I cannot be with you.

BROKEN PROMISES

In our divorce paperwork I made sure everything was documented and written down to cover and protect my sons. We are both supposed to keep the life insurance policies active in case anything happens to one of us, our children and the parent that is left alive will be able to take care of the children properly. Also, I made sure that the children are covered for sports and college. I will not be the only parent doing everything like I have been for the past 17 years.

Red Flag 2 is already at it with jezebel 2 for breaking promises and the divorce agreement. I can take him back to court and have him answer the judge why he has gone back against the divorce agreement. He can get into a lot of trouble with the courts. I have been very lenient, and I am not allowing him to get away with anything anymore.

Our middle child has now received his driver's license and we both promised him we will get him a vehicle. Red flag 2 said he can give me $3,000.00 towards the vehicle and I said I can do the same. Our son has held down an amazing gpa during the hell of the divorce and will go away to college in a year. Red flag 2 promised he has his portion but then spent it on his mistress for their wedding. My son was pissed but most of all heartbroken that his father had already gone back on his promise. I was forced to give my son my 2013 Toyota Highlander that I was going to trade in for my new 2022 Toyota Rav4. I was pissed as well because when we say we are going to do something for our children we do it. Now this ninja is here acting recklessly and hurting my sons just to please this jezebel 2. I told him I could not trade my vehicle in exchange for my new vehicle. I had to give the vehicle to my middle son. So, I bought the new vehicle using my own money. This is not the only thing Red Flag 2 has done.

Red Flag 2 and jezebel 2 had the audacity to ask my son to move out of his room to the basement so jezebel 2 daughter could move into his room. I lost it with that. If I had known he would move that hoe into my old house and mistreat my children this poorly, I would have made him sell the house in the divorce. My son was not happy and hurt again but trying to love his father. He has admitted his father has changed and he's really struggling to love him. My sons said they know they can always count on me, and they thank me as much as possible. I have addressed this to Red Flag 2 about him ruining his own relationship with his sons. I told him I will never cover for him again and he is the cause of everything.

God does not like ugly and he does not like when you do his innocent children wrong. Rule number one with me- DO NOT MESS WITH MY CHILDREN, MY GRANDDAUGHTER and MY DOG.

<u>JEZEBEL 2 STILL AT IT</u>

Stepparents can be good or bad. Unfortunately, my sons have a horrible evil person married to their father. This Jezebel 2 does not get the part of she is not my children's mother. She keeps stepping over the boundaries and you would think the Order of Protection and Restraining Order I have on her would make her realize something is seriously wrong with her and she needs help. This Jezebel 2 still going crossing the lines and this time impersonating to be my youngest son's mother with the school.

Let me explain exactly what happened. So, Jezebel 2 registered her daughter to go to the same school as my youngest son. During orientation being shown around Jezebel 2 brings up to my son's counselor that her son goes to the school as well and he is in seventh grade. The counselor asked who her son was and then she said my son's name. The counselor knows me very well and he knew she was not my youngest mother. Then she had the nerve to try and ask about his schedule and continue the conversation. The counselor did not discuss anything with her and called me right away to inform me of the situation that just occurred. The counselor said this is very disturbing that Jezebel 2 even tried to discuss anything and impersonate as his mother. I asked the counselor to put everything in writing and to not discuss anything with her and to notify all my son's teachers. If anything needs to be discussed regarding my children to now do a three-way conference call strictly between me and my children's father (red flag 2). I was livid and notified their father telling him he needs to get her under control, and he had the nerve to tell me don't talk to me about my wife. That is when I truly lost it on him. I told him when it has to do with someone impersonating me to claim to be my children's mother. Oh, I have every right to address him. See what you will not do is have someone out here trying to be me with my children. That is against the law trying to impersonate someone and on top of that Jezebel 2 works for the Buffalo school district. Now I have the letter from the school in my hands. I am speaking to the authorities to see what other actions I can take against Jezebel 2. I feel like I am living in fatal attraction because this person has some serious mental issues. My youngest son does not like her and has addressed this numerous times to his father way before they got married. It was to the point where his father hid the fact that they were getting married on the 4th of July and that was the holiday he had the boys.

Let me make this very clear to everyone, I am happy that I left this vindictive man, but I am not happy he is allowing an outsider to mistreat my son, overstep her place and I refuse for anyone to try and harm my children mentally or physically. Everyone deserves to be happy but if you're with someone who intentionally mistreats your children. Then you do not deserve to have any rights to that child. So yes, I do not like her, and I never will just on the strength of her hurting my son and trying to break his spirit. I am a mother first and I refuse not to protect my babies.

Parents: please protect your children from being bullied and that is with adults and children. We are supposed to protect our children from any hurt harm or danger. Now it is hard when they leave the house but when it is happening in your own home that is different. Pay attention and stand up for your children. Do what is right for them.

EDUCATION

To my brothers and sisters that are thinking about going back to school. Do not wait for the right time. Time is slowly slipping away, and we need to do everything we can before our time is up. Look at me, I went back to school scared and all at the age of forty-two, but I did it. I graduated with honors and made sure I gave it my all.

Allow me to tell you fully how and why I went back to school. So, I have been wanting to go back to school for years, but it was never the right time, or I allowed my ex to talk me out of it. Well that all changed, and I took that leap. God told me to go back to school and get my degree in law. So, when I signed up for college again, I decided since I am forty-two, I will just go for paralegal because becoming a lawyer takes years and being a paralegal was expensive. God told me don't worry about the finances I have you covered.

SIDE NOTE: when God sends you on a HIS mission, he will fit the bill and make sure everything is ready for you. All you must do is trust the process. Whew this is called that blind faith. Yes, I go scared and all with GOD, but I trust GOD with all my heart.

So back to the story. I went to Briarcliff college literally around the corner from my house at this time in 2016 and registered as a freshman. I had some credits that were transferred over but not many. So basically, I was starting all over again. I signed up for Paralegal classes. This was during the time I just was involved in a motor vehicle accident and was injured. So, I was home healing and doing therapy. So, I could take classes online and some on campus. The courses I took on campus were legal classes with the attorneys teaching. I am a visual and if I have questions I wanted to not have to wait for a response through an email. I needed the attorney to answer right then and there so my mind could be at ease.

After I signed up for classes and went home, all hell broke loose because Red Flag 2 did not want me to go back to school. I told him what God said and he still had a fit. I told Red Flag 2 I will be obedient to God, and I am staying in school. Our marriage was already on its last leg, and I refused to give in and not finish school. I needed to do that for myself as well as for GOD. I graduated with top honors with an overall GPA for the entire school year with a 4.90.

Graduation day was the best feeling ever to cross the stage and hear my sons screaming that's my mom. I showed my children no matter what age you are, always put your mind to doing something and conqueror it. I was showing my sons you can do anything you put your mind and heart to do.

<u>Communication</u>

Technology at this very moment in life has messed with how people communicate with one another. Before cellphones, we would use the home landline telephone to call someone, write a letter or we would go to their homes to have a conversation.

Now when you want to speak to someone you can text and not even call a person. Well for me, I like to talk on the phone, write letters and text when needed but to me it's so impersonal. When you're texting someone it's so impersonal.

Let's go back to memory lane for a moment

Remember growing up and having a crush on someone? We would write a note or letter to that person (ha, ha). Then either you give the letter directly to the person or to one of your friends to give to that person you were crushing on.

What about when you took a chance and walked up to the person and started a conversation just out of nowhere. Open communication verbally has seriously died out.

As a child growing up, we would play outside when the sun would be out and when it started to get dark, you knew it was time to head home. We used to go knocking on friends' doors asking if they could come out to play. Summertime was the best because we would meet up across the street at the playground and just be kids playing different games (hopscotch, double dutch, basketball, hide and go seek, duck duck goose, tag, red light green light, mother may I, freeze tag and so much more). Those were the good old days.

Let me ask you a question?

1. When it is time for dinner, do you have everyone gather at the table to eat together?

2. Do you hold conversations at the table while eating?

3. Do you have a policy No Cellphones at the table while eating?

I'm just trying to show you where the communication now has been lost at... In my house we all ate together and talked. My parents would ask how your day in school was, any homework, any problems with teachers etc. Then we would start talking about anything that comes up at the dinner table. We will start making plans for the weekend.

Let's start putting the phones down more and get group gatherings back. Let's start communicating more with less texting but more verbal conversation. The more we have open communication, the less stress people will have. Society has really changed for the worse in my opinion.

<u>THE ELDERLY</u>

When was the last time you sat down with the elders of your family and listened to the wisdom that came out of their mouths? When was the last time you stopped what you were doing and spent quality time with them?

As I sit here talking with my eighty-year-old grandmother, I am looking deeply into her eyes while she is speaking to me about her past. Things I did not know about and all she has endured through her lifetime. I am so thankful I still have her in my life and all she has done for me. In return I cherish her and help as much as possible. It is my turn to take care of her to my best ability, but the distance hinders me from taking care of her properly. I must rely and pray that the other family members will care for her the way I do and would if I was back on Long Island. Grandma's body is now fragile to the point where she can no longer do the things she used to do.

Allow me to paint a picture of what my grandmother used to do verses what can do at this stage in life. My grandmother grew up down south in Florida with her 12 other siblings. Growing up for her and her siblings was hard, but they pressed forward. Grandma used to work in a cotton field in that dead hot sun. Growing into a beautiful young adult my grandmother would go to the clubs, work to earn enough money to purchase her own house in Brentwood, New York years later.

When my grandmother moved to Brentwood, New York I was not born as of yet. Grandma would travel around the United States, a part of a union with her job and later because head leader of the 1199 union on Long Island. Grandma did not hold her tongue for anyone and most of all did not take anyone mistreating her in her personal life or business life. Grandma's essences and beauty captured many eyes along the way in her lifetime. Not many could keep up with her grind. Some say she intimidated men because of her being so outspoken verbally and never allowing anyone to walk all over her. Grandma and I would drive to Tennessee, Kentucky, Florida or we would be on a plane to another state.

When grandma was ready to go visit family, friends or associates, she wasted no time on making plans and then executing the plans to be realistic. Traveling with grandma was so much fun. I was the daughter she never had and when I say the love/bond we have still to this day cannot be broken. Now fast forward to the year 2022 as I describe the life changing lifestyle of my grandmother.

As I walk into the house that she has owned over 46 years in Brentwood, New York. Tears form to my eyes because of all the childhood memories that was created in her home. Now as I give her hugs/kisses I am making sure I am gentle, because her body is not the same anymore. Her body is fragile, wrinkled and aged many years. She can no longer get up so quickly or walk at a fast pace like before. Now she walks with a walker, in and out of hospitals, eyes not functioning properly as before. The old age has set in to the fact she no longer can drive and needs to wait on others. Being elderly has taken a toll on her physically and mentally. This woman used to be filled with so much life and excitement but now the light is dimming, and it breaks my heart. I know this is life and what to expect for getting older. I have tried to get her to move up to Buffalo for many years but had no luck convincing her to move. So tonight, I tried again to get her to move to Buffalo and live with me. This time she turned me down again but explained why. Grandma said if she moved out of her house that she has had over 46 years it would kill her. I said explain grandma because I do not understand. Grandma turned to me and said baby: you are my pride and joy along with my two sons I had but if I moved out of this house, I would die. I said don't say that grandma you still have more life in you. Grandma said baby if I left this house that I worked so hard for all those years ago, I really will die because I will be taken out of my element. I really felt what she was saying and the reason behind it.

I listened to every word she said and felt her pain. This is a woman who used to be free and loved life to the fullest. Now her body is breaking down slowly and deteriorating. The light is dimming slowly but surely. If you do not know how to do hair, then find someone who can come to the house and do their hair for them. If they need the lawn cut, find someone in the neighborhood who would like to make some money and cut the grass on a weekly basis. Find options that can help them and make them feel that they are still valued. Pick up the phone twice a week and talk with them and let them know you still value them.

Ladies & Gentlemen:

If you have a loved one and they are over the age of 60 please take the time out and cherish them. Be the driver for them if they longer can see properly. Be the housekeeper because they cannot move the way they used to. Be the ears to listen without responding because they want to be heard and not overlooked. Remember they used to take care of us when we could not do anything for ourselves. It is time to repay the favors of all the times the elders have taken care of us.

RACISM

<u>A Letter To My Brothers Of Color</u>

The color of our skin changes the dynamic automatically living in this cruel world. The time is 2022 and nothing has changed with how the public perceives my beautiful melon people. My brothers, I see your pain and all that you must endure after you leave your home each day. You are praying to make it back home safely because we are being hunted daily and killed because of our skin tone. It is an everyday battle just to show your intelligence and defend your thought process in return to the answers you submitted. No matter how much skills and education you carry, your skin tone is seen before you even speak a single word. Your resume can be so pristine but still you will get turned down for someone less educated Caucasian. The racism is bluntly in your presence daily, but still, you keep fighting to survive another day.

Society is cruel in so many aspects and when you think we have evolved here something smacks you in the face. Reminding you that you will never be considered equal just because of the color of your skin. Brother, I feel your pain and I am here to encourage you to keep your head up, keep pressing toward the mark of success. You may feel alone and defeated but you're not alone. Our skin tone is so amazing, embracing the beauty of our skin and all that our blood carries.

I know it is hard getting hit daily because of the fact your essence makes them fear you. My brother, you carry a lot of weight on your shoulders and need someone to help carry the heavy load. Always remember who you are and what you bring to the table. If they do not want you to eat with you, then create your own table and elevate your table to the greater success you can become. Iron sharpens iron and you need to make sure your team is solid as well.

Doors may get closed in your face because of your skin tone but you do not ever have to accept the closed doors. When one door closes, another shall open. Never give up, never forget who you are and what you are called to be. Remind them by using your intelligence against them in the business world. I can speak on this because I have three amazing sons I am raising. It is not easy having these talks with my sons about not being accepted in places just because of racism still exist in today's society. I have now given all three of my sons the talk no mother ever wants to speak on but is a must in an African American home.

<u>TALKING TO YOUR SONS & DAUGHTERS</u>

1. Make sure to always have your identification on you.
2. When entering the car place your insurance card and driver's license on the dashboard. Just in case you ever get pulled over it's in the police officers' eyesight.
3. If you get pulled over, make sure you roll down all the windows, place your hands on the steering wheel and if you have passengers in the vehicle. Make sure you have your passengers in the vehicle place their hands on the dashboard and head rest in front of them.
4. If you are the driver of the vehicle, make sure you tell your passengers to shut up and let you do all the talking. Because you need to get everyone home safely.
5. Do not make any sudden movements while speaking to the officer and look them in their eyes.
6. I know this is hard, but momma wants to make sure you make it home safely.
7. If anything goes wrong and you get arrested for no reason, ask for your phone call because that is your right and call me right away.
8. Do not sign or say anything else until your parent arrives at the precinct.

See this conversation must be discussed in an African American home just because of the color of our skin. This is sad we fear for our children's lives daily. No other race must deal with injustice by the police as much as we do. The African American community has always been under fire by the people, Caucasian civilians and it needs to stop. My family has been under fire by the police on several different occasions. Allow me to share my most recent encounter with the law.

THIS HAPPENED TO ME
TRUE STORY

I am going to share a few true story moments with you about a situation that occurred to me. Just let me first remind you, that I am a paralegal, podcast hostess, business owner and mother.

So, July 2022 I was flying back from North Carolina after having my book signing. I missed my connecting flight because the first flight was waiting for the pilots and the crew to arrive. The airport was able to get me on another connecting flight but would only fly into Rochester, NY and not the Buffalo airport. I was ok with that and said I will take a uber the rest. I needed to be at work the next morning and had no other choice. So, while I am waiting while the attendant makes my new ticket to board and Caucasian your female overheard, I needed to get to Buffalo, and she did as well. I did not know her, and she did not know me. This was our first time and she said if you do not mind miss, I will split the uber with you. LOOK AT GOD working this out already. So, we introduced ourselves to each other and because associates right away. We flew to Rochester, and I called the uber. (I have never done this before in my entire life, but I did not get any ill vibes from her).

We took the uber home and arrived at my house by 1:30 am. Now rule of streets for anyone that is African American you try not to be out past midnight to avoid any issues with the police. I had no choice but to be out. As we are traveling down Maple Road, Amherst, New York I see a police officer at the light on the opposite direction. I advised my passenger that we were about to be pulled over. She did not believe me and said Nicole why would the officer mess with you? I said Stacy because it is past midnight, and I am a colored female. Not even two minutes after I said that here comes the officer turning his lights on and pulled me over. I rolled down all the windows and told Stacy this is what we deal with on a daily basis. Stacy was so shocked and when the officer got out of his vehicle and flashed his light into the car. Stacy spoke before I could. Stacy addressed the officer and asked why did he pull us over? Stacy did not give the officer any time to speak because she hit him with a statement. Stacy said to the officer; Nicole was driving under the speed limit, and she is doing me a favor by driving me home after a long ordeal we just encountered. The officer was taken back and did not know how to respond. I now stepped in and addressed the officer.

I said good morning officer, how can I help you? The officer changed his focus on me and asked for my license and registration. Before taking my hands off the steering wheel, I addressed the officer and explained what I was about to do next. I said officer as you can see on my dashboard both my identification, insurance card and registration can be seen. I am going to take my right hand off the steering wheel to get them for you. Is that ok officer? The officer said yes, it is ok, and I retrieved the documents he requested. I then asked now please explain to me why I was pulled over. The officer didn't know how to address the situation and said oh your license plate light was out. That is when Stacy lost it and asked for his name and badge number. She apologized to me for the officer's behavior and said I should not have to deal with treatment like this from the police because of the color of my skin.

The officer stepped in and gave the documents back to me and asked where I worked at. I what does that have to do with you pulling me over? I said if you need to know I work for a Law Firm downtown Buffalo, NY. His eyes got big and said I will not give you a ticket. I said you could not give me a ticket even if you wanted to because a light bulb over one of my license plates cannot cause a ticket. I said officer I hope you have a better morning and be mindful of how you use your power because this morning situation was uncalled for. I took my documents from him, rolled up the windows and proceeded to take Stacy home. Stacy kept apologizing and I told her this is something I must live with. Is it right, HELL NO but this is what we face because of the authority they think they can abuse it. I keep in touch with Stacy.

Department Store:

My youngest son and I were at a department store walking around shopping. I noticed this man started following us. I wanted to make sure He was following us before I addressed him. We turned the corner and then doubled back and sure enough he was following us. I stopped and turned around and walked up to the man. I told him I did not appreciate him following me and my son. I advised we are not criminals, and we don't steal. I advised while you were watching me that Caucasian lady just stole 4 items. I advised you're so busy following a black person and losing sight on what's really going on. Don't you know he had the nerve to ask me to point her out. I said no and walked off to pay for our items.

Another incident dealing with the police. My second heartbeat was turning 13 and so we decided to have a birthday bash at the house. We had the DJ, photo booth, front and back yard was filled with teenagers and a great time. Some of the children, including my son, went to the gas station across the street to get some candy and were heading back to the house. This Caucasian did not have its pit bull on the leash and the children asked him to put the dog on the leash. This man came out his face cursing out the children and then commanding his dog to attack them. I was watching the children cross the street and hurried to see what was happening. By this time my husband at the time came over because I was calling his name along with my brother-in-law. The children were telling us what happened and all a sudden, a police officer pulls up to our house with the light flashing on our house.

Side note: I live in a residential neighborhood in Amherst and this man was treating us like we lived in the hood and we were less than criminals. That pissed me off to the fullest.

I told the officer to turn his light off and stop treating me and these children like we are the guilty party. I told the officer we were the victims and to show us some respect. He had the nerve to ask me who I thought I was. I told him the homeowner and a law-abiding citizen that's who. So, the officer then wanted to be condescending and that's when I shut him down. I told him who I work for and if I need to get one of the attorneys on the phone. He shut up then and started to act nicely. I made sure to report him the next day!

Again - Don't Start None Won't Be None! I don't play when it comes to me and the ones I love!

So, to all my people who are facing racism on a daily bases, you are anyone to try and make you feel less than.

WE ARE DOPE INDIVIDUALS & LOVE YOUR SKIN TONE!

BLACK IS BEAUTIFUL
YOU ARE VALUED
YOU HAVE PURPOSE

<u>THE POLICE KILLED MY UNCLE JOHN</u>

Still to this day our family really does not know what happened that night in Florida. All I knew was that my Uncle John was in his home and the police kicked in his door. The police opened fire and murdered my Uncle John. The police have not given us any answers nor a chance to look at the body cameras videos of that night.

When I say we speak of police brutality and the injustice all the time but when it hits your family it's a different kind of horrible feeling. This was one of my favorite uncles, and he always had a special name only he could call me. He was so down to earth and easy to talk with. My uncle never judged you but wanted to help you understand the family dynamics. Uncle John had this laugh that captured your heart, just a unique laugh and spirit. I truly miss him and his calling me that name. Nope I am not telling you his special nickname. That stays only in the family. Somethings must stay a secret lol.

Let me be very clear when I say this: we do have some good police officers but for the rotten officers that are still in the police force. Those rotten apples need to go because you cannot serve and protect but hate someone because of the color of their skin. As an officer of the law, you should not look at anyone any way but serve and protect.

MESSAGE

YOU WILL NEVER KNOW THE PAIN OF A BLACK PERSON IF YOU ARE NOT BLACK. YOU CAN NEVER SAY YOU KNOW HOW IT FEELS. GROWING UP WE PRAY THAT THE HATE WOULD GO AWAY BUT IT JUST KEEPS GETTING STRONG AND ITS SO SAD. WE WAS BORN A DIFFERENT COLOR AND BECAUSE OF THAT YOU FEAR US. IT MAKES NO SENSE AT ALL. WE ALL PUT ON OUR CLOTHES THE SAME WAY. WE ALL BRUSH OUR TEETH THE SAME WAY. WE ALL HAVE TO GO OUT AND WORK. SO WHY DOES THE COLOR OF OUR SKIN SCARE YOU SO MUCH?

I PRAY THAT RACISM ENDS! I PRAY THAT THIS WORLD CAN BE BETTER AND GET RID OF ALL THE HATE!!!

HEALTH ISSUES

ASTHMA AFTER COVID

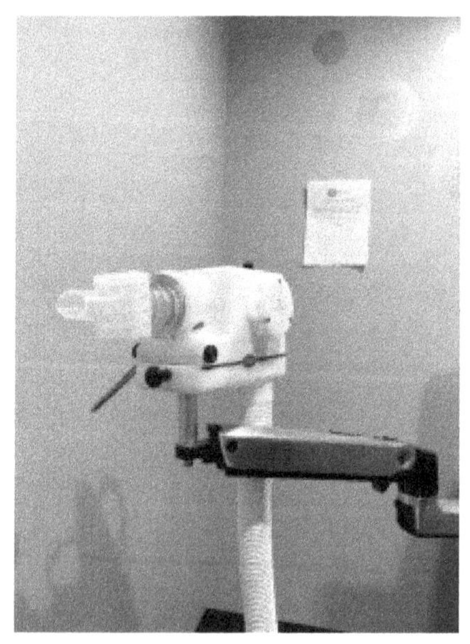

THE AFTER EFFECT

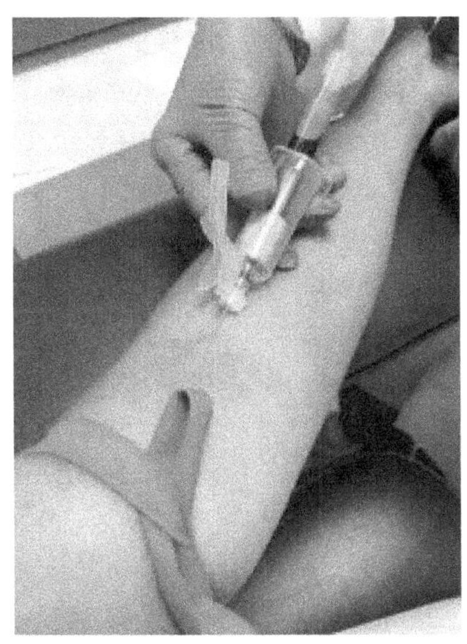

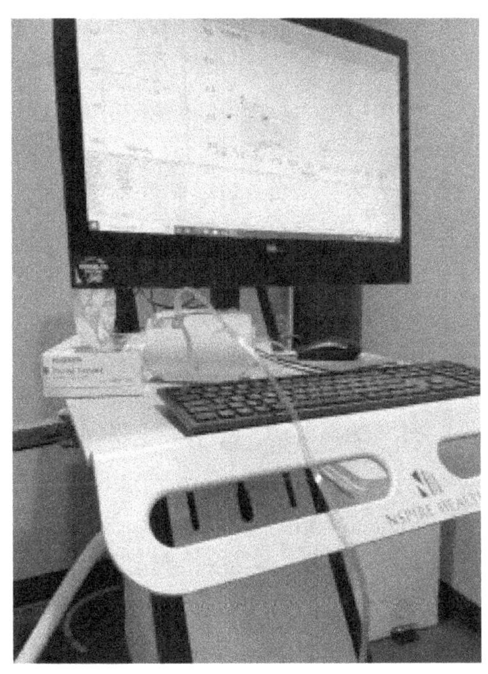

When COVID hit the United States in February 2019, we did not know the exact effect COVID would bring to the nation. Two (2) years later and the people are still trying to recover fully from the destruction it has caused to the economy, people's lives (financially and health wise).

I had acute asthma as a child growing up but now after having COVID I have full blown asthma. Lately if I get a cold and do not tend to it right away, it turns into bronchitis, and I now would need steroids to resolve my sickness. The cold goes right into my lungs and my breathing starts to become hard to breathe and the inhalers do not do much for me. I feel a weight on my chest and then the coughing starts controlling which is scary. So, this last March 2022 I was sick with a cold and the cough would not stop and it literally scared me and the children. I drove myself to Urgent Care because it is less of a weight compared to going into the hospital emergency room. So, while in Urgent Care they had to test me to make sure I did not have COVID again due to my symptoms. I told them I don't have COVID, but they still checked anyways. The results were negative and then I said can we get to the bottom of this. Urgent Care referred me to the Pulmonary specialist so we could figure out what is triggering my asthma attacks so much.

I met with one of the doctors in the Pulmonary department and we worked out a schedule for me to get blood work drawn, x-rays and breathing test. COVID activated my asthma from acute to now full-blown asthma, but we (the doctors & myself) wanted to make sure nothing else was damaged pertaining to my lungs. The doctor then scheduled for me to come back and go over the results. Thanking GOD that my results were great news but unfortunately, when I get a cold, I have to just get treatments for my breathing. COVID did not harm my lungs any further, but it is better to be safe than sorry.

The doctor has now prescribed an everyday inhaler to take in the morning to help open my lungs up. Since I have been using this inhaler once a day, I have not had to use my emergency inhaler unless I am running or walking at a fast pace.

I am thankful to have health insurance and most of all the doctor that I have listened to me. Not many doctors listen to the patient and try to tell the patient what is wrong with them. We need more doctors like the one I have.

MESSAGE: ALWAYS LISTEN TO YOUR BODY! IF SOMETHING IS WRONG WITH YOUR BODY, PLEASE GO GET CHECKED OUT RIGHT AWAY. DO NOT WAIT TIL IT IS TOO LATE.

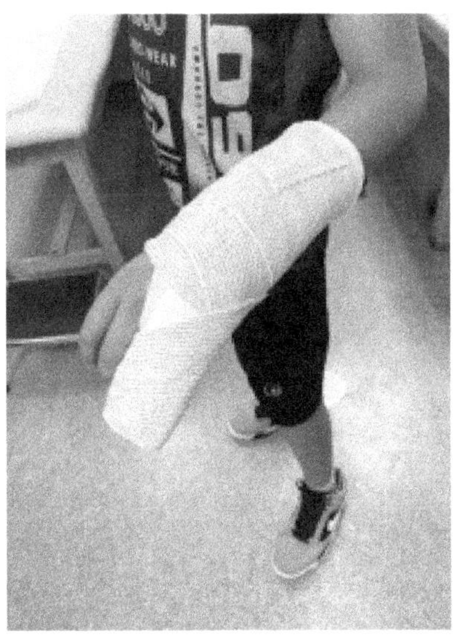

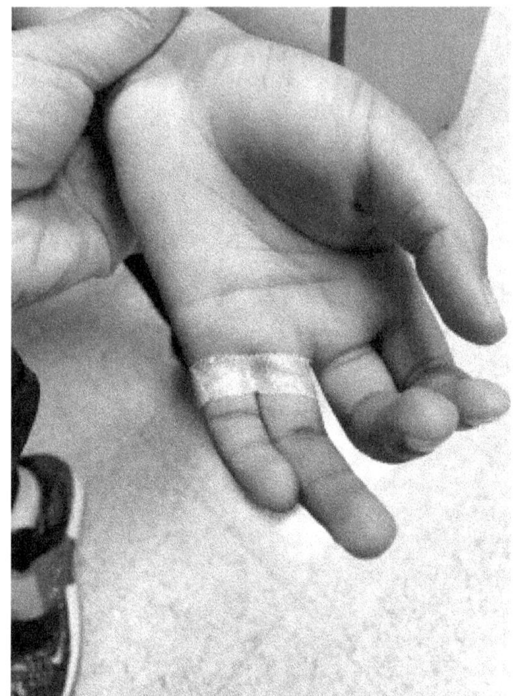

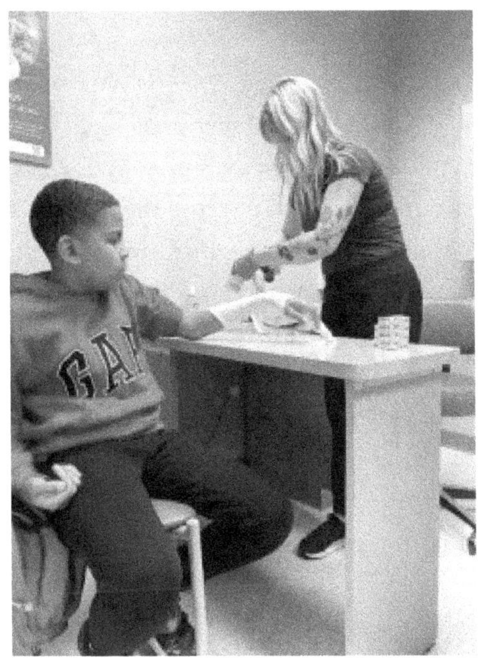

IT'S BROKEN
IT'S BROKEN - APRIL 23, 2022

Myles is the baby out of his other siblings and this boy has never had a dull moment of his life yet. From the time he was conceived this boy has been moving at his own pace and always active. Myles has always been passionate about sports and everything he does. Myles is an athlete of the highest level. When he steps onto the basketball courts or baseball fields, it's like a switch comes on and he gives the game all of him til the very end. His passion for the game and hunger to do better each game, each practice just fuels my fire as well. That's my baby and I love watching him and rooting him on from the sideline. I am his number one fan besides GOD. God named him WARRIOR and in Hebrew Myles name means just that.

Now let's get into the photos above and this long process of trying to contain an athletic son who has never had to endure sitting still for six weeks. I do not know if it was killing me more. So, allow me to tell you how this happened.

On April 23, 2022, at 5pm, Myles was playing with his travel basketball team. Myles received the basketball pass and then the opposing team member intentionally fouled Myles. Myles fell and as he was falling, Myles put his hand out to stop the fall to make it less painful when he hit the ground. As I am watching this play out right in front of me, I see my son falling and putting his hands out to break his fall. Well Myles left hand went first and his pinky went the opposite direction. Now let me explain something to you guys. Myles hardly cries when he gets hurt so if he is crying you know it is serious. The opposing team coach helped pick Myles off the floor and when Myles got up he started jumping up and down with tears in his eyes. I ran over ice and placed it on his hand. I took the ice off and noticed his pinky started to swell. I said to his father (RED FLAG 2) it is broken. His father did not believe me.

Side note: I have had my pinky broken when I was Myles age 11 and I know when a finger is broken)

I kept the ice on Myles hand, and I wanted to take him to get x-rays right away, but Myles did not want to leave his team. So, we stayed rooting for his team and then right after the game was over, I took him to the emergency room. His father kept saying I was over exaggerating, and I had to put him in his place. I told him don't tell me what I already know is true. I am a mother, and my mother has been a Registered Nurse for the past 40 years. I know a broken finger when I see one. I no longer gave him any response and hung up. So, we get to the emergency room, and we had 20 people ahead of us. I turned right around and went to Urgent Care on Sheridan Drive, Amherst, NY. We took our temperatures due to the pandemic everyone must get their temperatures taken before going any further. Myles was registered and now it was just us waiting for the doctor to have Myles get x-rays. Myles father called to check up on him saying it's just a sprain and you know your mother is over exaggerating. We kept his father on the phone so he could hear the results of the x-ray. The doctor confirmed my suspicions and said his pinky was broken but in the worst location. Myles broke his pinky in the growth portion of the pinky. Meaning if he did not get his pinky reset by an orthopedic specialist his pinky might not grow properly nor heal. Now remind you this game was on a Saturday evening. The doctor could not do anything but tape up his finger with a splint until we was able to see the specialist. The following day I called to make an appointment at Excelsior Orthopedics on Sheridan Drive, Amherst, NY. I love that place because they are friendly, showed my son so much compassion and tried to cheer him up.

Myles knew he was benched for six to eight weeks, and he did not like hearing those words. We are called in the back and here is how everything played out. The nurse took Myles for another x-ray to make sure they knew exactly how serious his break was and compared his break to the original x-ray that was taken two days before. The specialist came over and broke down the next procedures to all three of us: Myles, myself and his father. The doctor stated they must reset the broken pinky by first injecting Myles with a long needle to numb up the area but first they had to spray something over his hand to freeze it a little to help make the needle injection a little less painful. Well, when I tell you Myles took this like a champ when they injected his left hand near the broken finger like a champ. Myles squeezed his father's hand while I hugged him to give him my motherly love and comfort. We all watched the doctor inject the needle into his hand and blood started to come out and the doctor reassured us that this was natural to happen.

After the injection Myles had to wait thirty minutes for the hand to be numb. Once the hand was numb the doctor told us to brace ourselves because here comes the hard part for us. I said that wasn't enough; she said no, unfortunately, I now must pull and pop Myles finger back into the proper position. The doctor said this is the hard part ready one, two, three and the doctor pulled the finger, pushed the finger and reset the pinky. The nurse wrapped the two fingers together so the pinky would not be able to move and then the words that came out of her mouth were he must not do any and I mean nothing physically for the next eight weeks. Myles face dropped and said what? The doctor looked at us: mom and dad Myles cannot play any sports, no physical activities for the next eight weeks and we must bring him back in a few days to make sure the pinky is healing properly, or else surgery will be needed. So, for right now Myles will be in a soft cast so we can get to the pinky quickly if anything is wrong. I asked the doctor for a note for the school nurse and shared this news with all of Myles teachers and coaches. Myles was so down in his spirit because that meant no baseball nor basketball. Telling this boy to stay still was hard enough when he was younger and now that he plays all these sports, Myles does not know the word sit still. Well, his father and I looked at each other and said yeah this is going to be painful for all of us because this boy will make our lives hell till, he can play lol.

Myles thought he was slick by saying he wanted to go to practice to still be there for the team and help root them on for games. I gave him a try the first week and this boy blew it horribly. Let me tell you he was caught bouncing and passing the basketball with his right hand and then at baseball he was hit in the face by the baseball. I told Myles this is a serious matter and if his pinky does not heal properly then surgery it will be and that means a longer time being out of playing any sports. Myles knew I was ticked off, so I kept him from going to any practices or games for at least two weeks as his punishment for not taking this seriously. We had to do our follow up visits with the specialist every week and then we received the great news that the pinky healed properly, and Myles could go back on the court and field. We all felt like we were in jail with him, not being able to do hardly anything. He tried to make the best out of not doing anything physical that could harm his healing process.

That InGrown Hair Issue
Men & Women

Ingrown Hair: occurs when a hair that has been removed starts to grow back and curves into the skin. This normally happens after we have shaved, waxed or tweezered.

Now let's be honest here, those ingrown hairs hurt tremendously. If you do not pluck them right away it can cause a buildup and can be painful.

I had an issue in my late 20's with an ingrown hair in my left armpit. An ingrown hair formed, and the hair stayed under the skin and did not come to the surface. When I tell you guys the pain began a few days later. I used hot water on a towel thinking it can help reduce the bump that was forming more each day.

My mother said try the old school by peeling a potato and using the skin to help resolve this issue. That did not work either and it has now gone on for four days. I gave in and called the doctor's office to schedule an appointment. The doctor knew it was seriousness of this situation and he got me in the same day. Unfortunately, the doctor had to sterilize the area and make an incision in my left armpit. The doctor had to place a stent inside to help drain the bump fully. So much puss came out while the doctor made the incision. The stent had to stay in my armpit for a few days to make sure all was cleaned out fully and the issue would no longer occur. A week passed returning to the doctor to clean the stent and entire area for no infections. The doctor cleaned the area and withdrew the stent. I now have a scar under my left armpit as a reminder to never allow an ingrown hair to go untreated.

Men I did not forget about you trust me on that. We are grown so let's talk about the ingrown hair on the men's face and on the groin area. It is different for the men who shave below or sweat tremendously in the groin area. Sometimes you want to start fresh, or the hair has grown so wild that you're shaving or cutting the area low. Ingrown happens to us all so you should not feel ashamed or embarrassed. Women love a man that is well groomed and keeps up with their hygiene.

MORAL OF THE STORY HERE: ALWAYS INSPECT YOUR BODY AND MAKE SURE YOU TEND TO ANY INGROWN HAIRS RIGHT AWAY. IF THE PROBLEM CONTINUES DEFINITELY SEE A DOCTOR ASAP.

<u>KIDNEY STONES</u>

Kidney stones are caused by drinking little water, not exercising enough, obesity, weight loss surgery, eating foods with too much salt or sugar, infections, family history inherited.

Well, I had my first kidney stone ever in 2021 and that was a pain I wish never to experience again. The stone was a little big and I had to wait for it to pass. Listen everyone, I am writing to let you know this is serious because if the stone is too big you will need to have surgery to remove it.

Be careful what you are intaking into your body and what you are lacking in your body. Kidney stones can be passed down through the family blood line and on my father's side they get kidney stones a lot. So now I must be careful and make sure I am drinking my water a lot more and cutting back on the sweets. Being forty-five about to turn forty-six, I need to cut back on the sweets for sure. I have always had a sweet tooth.

Moral of the story.... Everyone please eat better and take care of yourself.

CODE OF THE STREETS

<u>LOYAL</u>: GIVING OR SHOWING FIRM AND CONSTANT SUPPORT OR ALLEGIANCE TO A PERSON OR INSTITUTION!

<u>SOLID</u>: SOMEONE YOU CAN ALWAYS COUNT ON!

<u>RELIABLE</u>: CONSISTENTLY GOOD IN QUALITY OR PERFORMANCE; ABLE TO BE TRUSTED

<u>TRUST</u>: FIRM BELIEF IN THE RELIABILITY, TRUTH, ABILITY OR STRENGTH OF SOMEONE OR SOMETHING!

<u>FIRM</u>: HAVING A SOLID, ALMOST UNYIELDING SURFACE OR STRUCTURE. STRONGLY FELT AND UNLIKELY TO CHANGE.

<u>UNYIELDING</u>: NOT GIVING WAY TO PRESSURE; HARD OR SOLID (A PERSON OR THEIR BEHAVIOR) UNLIKELY TO BE SWAYED.

<u>DEVOTED</u>: VERY LOVING OR LOYAL

LISTEN: they do not make many of us like this anymore. I was raised old school and I am raising my children that way as well. Our word is our bond, and we are loyal till we see the same energy is not given back. Once you show me that I can no longer trust you or rock with you, I wipe my hands and keep it moving. My time is too precious to deal with drama I did not cause. Now if I caused something I will try to fix it.

Now reading those words on this page: Do you fit that category? Can your circle say they trust you? If not, then look at yourself and fix what needs to be changed. I'm just saying: people do not want to have to second guess if you're a friend or a snake. Yeah, I said it and I am not sugaring coating anything for anyone. That is the problem with society today. Everyone wants to walk on eggshells when speaking on topics. Nope you need to hear the real deal and face the music as they say. Check yourself and correct yourself, be an adult and own your actions.

<u>CHILDREN ARE OFF LIMITS</u>

I was raised differently and in a different era, but I will pass this down from one generation to another. **CHILDREN ARE OFF LIMITS!** That means no adult should be putting a child in grown folks' business. No child should be in the middle of parents arguing and knowing what's taking place. No child should be told not to tell the other parent what's going on in their home if it is not safe for them. Our children should be protected, shown proper guidance, and loved.

See the problem today the elders have gone to glory and this new generation is not following the old traditional values of honoring these children and keeping them safe. Well, for me and my house I make sure my children are protected as much as possible and I will fight to keep them safe. I will fight to make sure they have a happy and safe childhood. We cannot control the outside world, but we damn sure can control what goes on in our children's homes as parents.

Parents, you should want nothing but the best for your children and for their mental state as well. No parent should force a child to do something that harms them mentally or physically. If a child says they feel uncomfortable around a person, please respect that, and pay close attention. Parenting is not easy, but you should take one day at a time and learn as you go. We should want to create great memories with our children so they can pass it down to their children and so on. Create great values and memories for our children, grandchildren, great greats and so on.

So, the next time you decide to do anything regarding your children, please think first before acting.

<u>WHEN THEY SWITCH UP ON YOU</u>

Let's start addressing these types of people in your life. We have all had them and I am included. Real talk! Everything can be going so well with a person and then out of nowhere they stop texting, calling you back and ignoring you. Now it will only take me two times to reach out and I will address it: hey you good? Did I offend you? See I am mature enough to ask because I was raised properly. If I value friendship, I want to make sure everyone is good in my camp. Now when I ask it is genuine but don't come with lies after I ask you. Once you lie to me, it's a wrap because that means you cannot be mature enough to admit if something was wrong. Seeing that right there makes me then question was it all fake from the start.

Anyways, when people switch up on you it's all good. Do not sweat the small stuff and I know that can be hard at times. Trust me, I get it and have had to deal with people that switched up on me. What I am speaking about is basically from experience. Every time I try to figure out a person back in the day would give me a headache. I stopped trying to figure out people and just thank God for removing that person. God saw something I didn't, and He is just protecting me from whatever schemes they were plotting or maybe down the line hurt that would have come out of the situation if it began to form. Now do not misunderstand what I am saying. It hurts losing people you started to trust. Always remember some people come into your life for a season or lifetime. When their time is up God moves them along or moves you along. Either way their time is up and you just need to dust your shoulders off and keep it moving. Like grandma always say: Can't cry over spilled milk, what is done is done baby.

Now if you were solid and loyal to them and they switched up. It is their loss and not yours. Remember that. Do not ever lose sleep over someone walking out of your life. It will mess with your health and mind. Grandma always said: You reap what you sow, and God will handle anyone that mistreats you. Leave it with God and keep living life to the fullest. Don't do to others that you would not want done to you. I live by that saying. I treat others how I want to be treated but I had to learn don't expect me from others.

Message: Be true to who you are, and God will give you the proper circle of friends you can trust and have your back. Stay focus and stay in Gods face. Some journeys you must walk alone, and you

will have to be okay with that. Not everyone is your friend, and you must really guard your heart.

I AM STILL STANDING

Have you ever been knocked down, talked about, disrespected, mistreated, not loved, betrayed, cheated on, abandoned, lied to, used, and abused?

We all have had one of these things happen to us, but you know what? YOU ARE STILL STANDING! You are still living, and you have purpose. Don't you dare let the faults of others tear you down or try to break you.

I want you to speak life over yourself daily. Look in the mirror each day and night or how often you need to do this but SPEAK LIFE.

SPEAK LIFE.... SAY THIS WITH ME......

I AM BEAUTIFUL OR HANDSOME (WHATEVER GENDER YOU ARE)

I AM IMPORTANT

I LOVE ME

I AM A SURVIVOR

I AM GODS CHILD

I AM ENOUGH

I AM SOMEBODY

I MEAN SOMETHING

I AM SMART

I AM AWESOME

I AM PROUD OF ME

DON'T WAIT FOR ANYONE TO VALIDATE YOU! GOD HAS ALREADY DONE THAT. DO NOT WORRY WHAT OTHERS THINK OF YOU. BE THE BEST VERSION OF YOU DAILY. KEEP REINVENTING YOURSELF FOR THE BETTER. KEEP PUSHING/MOVING FORWARD. REACH FOR THE STARS AND DO IT WITH EXCELLENCE! DO NOT GIVE UP ON YOURSELF! TAKE THE SHOT! I BELIEVE IN YOU!!

I AM PROUD OF YOU!

LOVE EXERCISE:

I really want you to take the time out and meditate on each question below before answering. Yes, we know everyone has a love language but first you must see if you really can identify love. People say they know love but now it is the time to really see.

1. Does anyone really know the true meaning of love?
2. What is love to you?
3. Do you know how to love?
4. Do you know how to accept the love that is given?
5. Who was the first person you can say you truly loved and why? Now was that love?
6. Do you tell the ones you love that you love them often?
7. Can your loved ones feel your love?

I bring this topic up because this world is missing LOVE. This world and the people in this world need real love. SO many are broken and walking around lost because of the lack of true genuine love. It is time to heal and bring love back into our lives fully and completely. Our children need love, our families need love, our streets need love, our court rooms need love, the jails need love.

Father God, I pray right now for the person reading this message about love. Father touch this person fully and completely in all aspects of their life. Father if they are lacking in love in any part of their spirit, I ask that you breathe on them and move in a mighty way. Give them the love that they need. Heal the parts that may be hurting. Father allow your will to be done in them and through them. Allow them to touch others in a positive way and pay this forward. Father, we thank you in advance of what you're doing and about to do. Thank you, GOD, for your unconditional love and protection. This is my prayer for your children of this world.

WOMEN IN THE WORKING FIELD

The hypocrisy in the working field towards women simply put ridiculous and I'm sick of it. Why is it ok for a man to be working and not get the same treatment as it is given to us female workers? Working and being a mother is very hard because we want to be at the top and juggle being a hands-on mother as well.

I'm going to speak only for me and if this applies to you then you can relate. I have been working since I turned eleven years old. The more driven I was to be successful the more passionate I became towards sharpening my skills in society. Now that I am an adult, mother, grandmother and business owner. I am juggling motherhoods, entrepreneur, have some me time and relaxing time. Yes, this is very demanding but one thing for sure – I AM MOM first no questions asked! I am at their games rooting my babies on, flying across the world on business and giving back to my community as much as possible.

Now here is where I disagree with employers. All employees:

1. Everyone should have 10 sick days for the year
2. One year working at the job you get a week off
3. Working two years you get two years off
4. Working five years at an employment you should have three weeks off for vacation.
5. You should be able to work one day from home each week.

The way the pandemic has attacked this economy, I feel if it is a corporation and we can work from home, then why shouldn't we. If I am not healthy my family will suffer and that is my main concern. Let's be real with employers, they will replace you really quick, but your family cannot do that. You must think about your home before work at times and it's sad. I feel the companies do not have the proper compassion for their employees and they are being selfish. So many people are not working today in fear of going outside because of all these new diseases now appearing.

Let's talk about the daycare fees. Thank goodness my children no longer need daycare, but the fees are ridiculous. Parents are working to pay for childcare and barely have enough to live off what they receive as a paycheck. Why don't corporations have daycares in the building so the parents can see the children on their breaks and make it reasonable for the children to be in the building. Help the families that are working for the company.

So again, tell me why must we go into the office when we can work from home? I pray the corporations, firms, courts & schools think about this. I do not mind doing virtual schooling and working from home. Something to think about now a days.

SOCIETY

77

BUYING A HOUSE IN 2022
What you need to buy a house:

1. Good credit
2. Bank statements of all your accounts
3. The last 3-6 months of paystubs
4. Make sure your credit cards have been paid up to date
5. Proof of a pre-approval mortgage
6. Do not close any credit cards out because you will keep your credit score go down tremendously. Keep them open but at a zero balance if possible

In 2006 when we brought the house society was not as hectic nor was it dealing with a pandemic. Interest rates have now skyrocketed in 2022 with the pandemic everything has doubled in value and price. I am looking for a three-to-four-bedroom house with a nice size property and people have bid over me and over $100,000.00. I refuse to ever go back into debt, and I will just wait for the housing rates to drop back into the regular rates.

When I first started looking for a house it was in March 2022 and the interest rates were 3.6% and that was great with my credit score being a 723. I found a few beautiful homes but then others were out bidding me from every direction. I took it as a sign from God that it was not meant to be yet. Months have passed and I got frustrated and stopped looking for a little while. Now I am going to wait a year til the rates drop again. I have other important things to get ready for.

The moral of this story do not put yourself in debt or live over your means. Know your limit and just wait on Gods timing.

Keep looking and when God says that's the house, then that's when you will have no problems at all purchasing the house.

PURCHASING A NEW VEHICLE

In this time as well, the pandemic has really messed a lot of things up in this world. You can no longer walk into a car dealers lot and purchase a brand-new vehicle. You must order your vehicle and wait for the factory to assemble the vehicle then ship it. The factory is short of car chips, and it has become a major issue across the world.

So many steps now for purchasing a vehicle. You can either build your vehicle on the website of the factory or you can go to the dealer and buy your vehicle from the dealer. After the vehicle has been shipped them, that is when you receive your license plate and registration from the dealer. You do have to pay and have your insurance ready to be put on the vehicle the day of pick up.

<u>DRIVING</u>

Listen, I feel as I get older these people do not know how to drive. I feel people need to go back to driving school to get an updated version on how to be on the road.

Rules Of The Road:

1. Adjust your mirrors
2. Make sure nothing is blocking your views
3. Look both ways before pulling out
4. Look both ways before backing out
5. Signal when turning a head of time and not when you get to the spot your turning into (that ticks me off real quick)
6. Don't take forever to turn
7. Stop letting everyone out onto the main road!
8. On the highway don't be in the left lane going slow!!! It's the fast lane for a reason

9. Don't cut people off because that's how you can get cursed out
10. When you get into an accident call the police and exchange information at the scene!
11. Take photos if you have an accident of both vehicles
12. Stop having your dogs on your lap while driving
13. Look before changing lanes

Driving on the highway gets so frustrating because people don't look, or they switch lanes without looking. A lot of accidents are caused because of careless driving. It seriously needs to stop!

I'm going to share with you a true story about an incident that occurred in Shirley, NY when my oldest was 5 years old. I was driving down Williams Floyd Highway in Shirley one afternoon and that's a dangerous highway. Cars speed up and down that highway all the time and major accidents occur on that highway. So, I am in the left lane and this man makes a right turn onto the highway and then automatically tries to switch into my lane without looking. They almost hit my vehicle. I'm blowing the horn and so I swerved so they wouldn't hit me. Now I'm mad because they would have hit the side my son was on. We get to the light and I'm flipping on them. Don't you know this woman throws a pen at me from the passenger seat. I looked at her like a bull that saw red. I got out of the car and told her a piece of my mind and the driver that he almost hit me. He had the nerve to say I should have moved over for him. **I told the man it's only** 2 lanes idiot where was I going to do move off the road. I told the man he needs to learn how to drive, and I looked at his wife and told her if she wanted to keep her hand then she better not ever throw anything at me or anyone else ever again! He apologized for her and his behavior. I told him he would have hit my sons part of the vehicle and it that happened oh they would have had a serious problem then. I don't play when it comes to my children. They are special cargo and I value their lives more than mines when it comes to them.

Moral of the story- watch the road and drive properly because too many people are dying because someone is driving reckless! We all want to make it home safely!

Why Are Birthdays Important to me?

1. You made it another year
2. You still have breath in your body
3. You still have work to do here on earth

I celebrate others because you never know what they may be dealing with. Remember to treat people how you want to be treated. Many do not have anyone celebrating them and a nice shout out can go a long way to them. Always remember it could be you not waking up! It could be you being celebrated. It could be you alone. It could be you, so show Compassion as much as possible.

CELEBRATE

Today and every day I will celebrate life and all that I have. I am blessed to live and see my forties when others I grew up did not make it past the age of twenty-four. I embrace the good, bad and ugly but most of all I am living fully. I refuse not to be happy and not celebrate myself or others.

That is the problem with the world today. This world is losing compassion within themselves and spreading it onto the world. I do not want to walk around this earth bitter, evil, and empty. I will smile at anyone I meet and try to spread the love of Christ as much as possible. I smile and try to laugh through my painful days as well. I refuse to allow the enemy of this world to make me bitter.

So, when you see me celebrating someone else, try to pay it forward as well. I am trying to be the example I want to see in this world. It all starts with a smile or hello. It really is not that hard. Try it and be that change we need in this world. When you are no longer breathing on this earth, don't you want to be able to say I did my part on trying to make this world a better place. Once we are six feet underground, we cannot do anything else.

DEATH

<u>Death:</u> the action or fact of dying or being killed; the end of the life of a person or organism. Death comes at any given moment and can hit you in a different way each time. See you never know how you will respond until it happens to you.

When was the first time you experienced death hitting your family? How did you handle it? Do you still think of that person? Do you have unanswered questions that still linger in the back of your mind? Life happens and we know when you are born the end game is that we all must die at some point, but we are never prepared. As I grow older in age, I reminisce on the ones we have lost along the way. The memories that pop up are good/bad/sad, but I am thankful to have them to think back on. Some people that have left this earth hold a special portion in my heart and mind forever.

As I sit here typing tears are flowing down my face because I am thinking about so many loved ones. Everyone that holds a special part in my heart will be talked about. I will always keep them alive because they meant a great deal to me.

Please cherish the ones you hold dear to your heart. Make memories and take lots of photos. Photos will allow you to be able to look back on those special moments you captured. So, when you start to forget what that person looked like, you have the photos to help you.

I am so thankful to God for allowing me to keep the memories so fresh in my mind and spirit of the ones I love and miss dearly. Let us keep their memories alive and tell our children about them.

Thank you for your support and rooting for me. I appreciate every one of you. All my books can be found on Amazon and my website: www.godsproperty2022.com[1]. I can be reached on all platforms: Instagram, Facebook, Twitter. Allow me to help you free yourself and live fully. Subscribe to my websites to be updated on the newsletters and more to come. Stay tuned......

Most Heavenly Father as this reader finished this book, I pray this has resonated something in them. Allow them to apply this to their daily life. Father allow them to look at others in a different light and most of all allow them to soar in all aspects of their life. Father, we ask that you speak to each person as they can receive this book and all in it. Thank you in advance for what you're doing in our lives and on the work force. Holy Spirit keep moving and speaking as you see fit. In Jesus name AMEN!

BE BLESSED AND GO FOR IT ALL! WE ONLY HAVE ONE LIFE TO LIVE!

---

1. http://www.godsproperty2022.com